Love on Purpose
Plain and Simple

Tyson Canty

Love on Purpose: Plain and Simple

Copyright © 2016 Tyson Canty

All rights reserved. No part of this publication may be reproduced, stored in a retrieval system, or transmitted in any form or by any means – for example, electronic, photocopy, recording – without the prior written permission of the publisher. The only exception is brief quotations in printed reviews.

For information about special discounts available for bulk purchases, sales promotions, and educational needs, contact Tyson Canty at http://oneneighbor.net.

All Scripture quotations, unless otherwise indicated, are taken from the New King James Version®. Copyright © 1982 by Thomas Nelson. Used by permission. All rights reserved.

Cover design by Tyson Canty. Cover image by us.fotolia/NataArt

ISBN-13: 978-0-692-74587-8

DEDICATION

I would like to dedicate this book to the man who has always had my affection since we were 17 years old. It was then God showed me you were to be my husband. Eighteen years later, all I can say is "God is faithful!" Thank you for being my best friend, confidant, background singer to my random songs, husband, number one encourager of all of my endeavors. I love you.

CONTENTS

	Acknowledgments	i
1	The Foundation of Our Purpose	1
2	Love Is	9
3	Loving God: Learning to Love the Purpose-Giver	14
4	Loving You: You Are Worth It	23
5	Loving Others: Making Disciples	29
6	Keep Love Forever Present	34

ACKNOWLEDGMENTS

First, I would like to thank my childhood Pastor, Dr. Donald D. Ford I, for challenging me to discover my spiritual gifts and the call God has on my life. You saw beyond my speech impediment, taught me the fundamentals of preaching and teaching, and gave me opportunities to stretch, grow, and develop biblical aptitude.

Second, I would like to thank my mother for taking me to church as a child, being my first Sunday School teacher, and cultivating my desire to read God's Word.

CHAPTER 1
THE FOUNDATION OF OUR PURPOSE

Do you know your purpose, the reason God gave you the gift of life? Do you want to know what that purpose is? It is not until you give yourself completely to God that your purpose is revealed. And it is the more we give over to God and love Him the more of our purpose is revealed every day.

Purpose is defined as "...the reason why something is done or used: the aim or intention of something..." (Merriam-Webster). Everything we do should be on purpose and with intention – even the smallest and shortest of plans and goals. For example, you intentionally wake up and get ready for work one to two hours before your start time so that you can arrive on time. You have a purpose or intent as to which color M&M or Starburst candy you eat first. Just as your reasoning for why or how seems simple to you, God's purpose for us is not as complex as we tend to make it.

When we come to God to inquire of our purpose typically we have already searched and failed. It is one of the few times we come to God and actually want Him to tell us what to do. We are asking Him for a command and to direct our path. Just as He

---

By permission. From Merriam-Webster's Collegiate® Dictionary, 11th Edition ©2016 by Merriam-Webster, Inc. (www.Merriam-Webster.com)

commanded the sun and the moon where to hang in the sky and where to hide until their appointed time to shine, we want God to command us where to stand and how to walk into our destiny. You will find numerous commandments given by God. A commandment is defined as nothing more than a command, which is an order given to a person to do something. A command essentially is a purpose which must be fulfilled. There are only two that Jesus says are the greatest.

Before we take a look at those commandments, let us return to our previous question: Do you know your purpose? The answer is simple. You were made to love and be loved. We were all made in God's image. God is love (1 John 4:8). Jesus said in Matthew 22:37-40, "'You shall love the LORD your God with all your heart, with all your soul, and with all your mind.' This is the first and greatest commandment. And the second is like it: 'You shall love your neighbor as yourself.' On these two commandments hang all the Law and the Prophets."

Just as God is three persons in one, your purpose is also intertwined with three – God, you, and others. Your purpose first and foremost is love. Without love, nothing we do means a thing (1 Corinthians 13:2).

The Two Greatest Commandments
It is important that we get a firm grasp of what the two greatest commandments really mean because they make up the foundation for which our purpose is built. Jesus is recorded again in Mark 12:30-31 giving the two greatest commandments, "'And you shall love the Lord your God with all your heart, with all your soul, with all your mind, and with all your strength.' This is the first commandment. And the second, like it, is this: 'You shall love your neighbor as yourself.' There is no other commandment greater than these." The importance of the first commandment is obvious, or so we think. And, the second commandment may cause a few to scratch their heads and ask why Jesus emphasized the importance of loving our neighbor. Jesus was not ambiguous when He told us to love our neighbor, but said we should love our neighbor as

ourselves. It is more than just offering a vigorous wave from afar. Both commandments seem simple at first glance, but both come with a hefty price that some are not willing to pay – self-sacrifice.

First of the Greatest Commandments

Let us explore the greatest of all commandments in Mark 12:30, "And you shall love the Lord your God with all your heart, with all your soul, with all your mind, and with all your strength," or in other words love God completely, utterly and entirely with our whole being. It sounds straightforward. What does it actually mean to love God? Jesus said in John 14:15, "If you love Me, keep My commands." He goes on to say in verses 23 and 24, "If anyone loves Me, he will keep My word; and My Father will love him, and We will come to him and make Our home with him. He who does not love Me does not keep My words; and the word which you hear is not Mine but the Father's who sent Me." It is through our obedience to the Lord that we express our love for Him. However, let us refer back to the scripture; this obedience must take place in our heart, soul, mind, and strength.

Obedience in Your Heart

How do we obey the Lord with our heart? Luke 6:45 reads, "A good man out of the good treasure of his heart brings forth good; and an evil man out of the evil treasure of his heart brings forth evil. For out of the abundance of the heart his mouth speaks." If we dwell on evil thoughts or hold onto bitterness, hate, unforgiveness, among other negative emotions in our heart, eventually they will come out in our speech. The condition of our heart is important to God. It is the ultimate litmus test and the mirror God peers into to see the motivations of our actions. Proverbs 23:7 reads, "For as he thinks in his heart, so is he..." You may have heard the saying, "actions speak louder than words," but as we all know at times we have all said and done things that were contrary to our heart, which include our passion and motivation. When we would rather stay home and do nothing, we have agreed to go to the movies, grocery store, babysit, or help with housework. Our heart simply was not in it, but we did it anyway.

Unbeknownst to us, our true feelings might have showed in our expression or in our lackluster attempt to please the other person. We should apply this same awareness when we come to God in prayer, praise, worship, etc. God knows our heart. He knows if we are sincere. In all situations, we should first be sure our motivations are right and that our actions and speech line up.

Obedience in Your Soul

Our soul is the essence of who we are. It is our personality or character. You have heard someone described as having a *kind* soul or *gentle* spirit. These individuals are genuinely considerate and always thinking of others. They may even be known to diffuse conflict and encourage whenever the opportunity presents itself. When we obey God in our soul, our personality and character traits will align with God's will and His Word. God made us all different. We are not supposed to reconstruct our personalities, but to allow God to mold us. For example, as a child someone might be described as having a *bold* personality. The child could be said to be a natural born leader. How can they reign in this characteristic and display obedience to God? As a natural leader what better way to lead than to do so while displaying the characteristics of Christ. To be bold is to stand up for what is right regardless if it is popular or not (Acts 4:29). A bold leader will forgive when the world says it is okay to hold a grudge (Ephesians 4:32), remain faithful when it is easier to change loyalties (Proverbs 3:3-4), show compassion when indifference is common (1 John 3:17), walk with determination and enduring to the end when quitting is cheaper and less time consuming (2 Timothy 4:7-8). The list goes on and on. All of us have the ability to demonstrate many characteristics of Christ.

Obedience in Your Mind

Why does it matter what we think? Isn't obedience in our actions sufficient? No, your mind is the seedbed of your thoughts which dictate or influence your actions, mood, and emotions. Thoughts can take root and if allowed to grow and bloom can either be the motivation we need to progress or the obstacle that stands in our way. We cannot obey God if our thoughts keep us from living out His Word.

According to 2 Corinthians 10:5, we must take every opportunity in "casting down arguments and every high thing that exalts itself against the knowledge of God, bringing every thought into captivity to the obedience of Christ." We need to analyze every thought that enters our mind and ask: Is it negative, depressive, argumentative, anxious, evil, or the like? If so, it needs to be uprooted and replaced immediately with a truth of God before it is allowed to impact your thoughts, actions, or mood long-term. Have you noticed the more you dwell on a past mistake and beat yourself up, it lengthens the amount of time it takes to get out of that mental funk? It has the potential to affect your daily routine. You might stay inside the house rather than go to a garage sale, farmer's market, gym or sporting event and enjoy the day. Instead of thinking what a horrible person you are or what a stupid mistake that was, replace it with a truth, such as, "The steps of a good man are ordered by the LORD, and He delights in his way. Though he fall, he shall not be utterly cast down; For the LORD upholds him with His hand" (Psalm 37:23-24).

Remember no one is perfect. Though you may make a mistake do not let your thoughts keep you from moving forward in Christ in obedience. Learn from your mistake, repent, dust yourself off, and meditate on God's Word to keep your thoughts in check. Philippians 4:8 reads, "Finally, brethren, whatever things are true, whatever things are noble, whatever things are just, whatever things are pure, whatever things are lovely, whatever things are of good report, if there is any virtue and if there is anything praiseworthy – meditate on these things."

Obedience in Your Strength

With all of our strength or physical power, we are to obey God. Our physical power is essentially our physical body. With our body we carry out many actions and utterances. It is with our bodies that we are able to display outwardly to others what motivates us (heart), our character (soul), and what we think (mind), which is why it is important that all of these line up with God's Word so that we can always put our best foot forward and introduce others to the God we love and serve.

According to Merriam-Webster, to obey is simply "to follow the commands or guidance of..." and "...to conform to or comply with..." In everything we do and with our entire being, we are to follow the commands and guidance of God and to conform and comply with His instruction, which is His holy Word. This is how we demonstrate to God how much we love Him.

Second of the Greatest Commandments

Jesus told the disciples that the second greatest commandment is: "You shall love your neighbor as yourself" (Mark 12:31). In this simple command the word *as* stands out. According to Merriam-Webster, the word *as* means "...to the same degree or amount..." Quite simply put, the love you have for yourself should be the same love you have for others. Our love for one another should not be based on any external factors, such as, politics, finances, location, social status, past mistakes or accomplishments. Neither should our own personal grievances or prejudices affect the degree to which we love. In like manner, we should also afford ourselves these same leniencies and love ourselves unconditionally so that we can give that same love to others.

The Ten Commandments

What makes the two greatest commandments so great? They encompass the essence of the Ten Commandments (Exodus 20). If you look closely, you will see that Commandments 1-4 deal with the divinity of God and how God wants us to respect Him and His divine order for our lives. Commandments 5-10 describe the manner in which we are to conduct ourselves with one another and how God wants us to interact (Canty).

By permission. From Merriam-Webster's Collegiate® Dictionary, 11th Edition ©2016 by Merriam-Webster, Inc. (www.Merriam-Webster.com)

Canty, Pastor E.F. Interviewed by Tyson Canty. Personal Interview. Overland Park. September 15, 2013.

How we should relate to the divinity of God
Commandments 1 – 4
1. You shall have no other gods before Me (Exodus 20:3).
2. You shall not make for yourself a carved image – any likeness of anything that is in heaven above, or that is in the earth beneath, or that is in the water under the earth; you shall not bow down to them... (Exodus 20:4-6)
3. You shall not take the name of the LORD your God in vain... (Exodus 20:7)
4. Remember the Sabbath day, to keep it holy... (Exodus 20:8-11)

How we should relate to each other
Commandments 5-10
5. Honor your father and mother, that your days may be long upon the land which the LORD your God is giving you (Exodus 20:12).
6. You shall not murder (Exodus 20:13).
7. You shall not commit adultery (Exodus 20:14).
8. You shall not steal. (Exodus 20:15).
9. You shall not bear false witness against your neighbor (Exodus 20:16).
10. You shall not covet your neighbor's house; you shall not covet your neighbor's wife... (Exodus 20:17)

It is easy to see the parallel between the Commandments 1-4 and the first greatest commandment which sums up how we are to approach God and His divine nature. Similarly, there's an equal parallel between Commandments 5-10 and the second greatest commandment as it sums up how we are to treat one another on earth. Throughout the Bible, we see the main focuses of the two greatest commandments echoed in both the Old and New Testaments.

Chapter 1 Reflection Questions

1. What are three things you do intentionally (on purpose) everyday to show your love toward God or others?
2. In which areas do you struggle the most with obedience – your heart, soul, mind, or strength? What steps will you take to do better in these areas?
3. Looking at the Ten Commandments, do you fall short more with how you relate to the divinity of God or to others?
4. Say a prayer asking God to help you intentionally walk in obedience and relate to others according to His will and with love. Use your responses to questions 2 and 3 to align your prayer to your specific needs.

CHAPTER 2
LOVE IS

Love. Love. Love. Just like the name of God, love should not be used in vain or recklessly tossed around, but held in reverence and used with sincerity. In this world, love is the difference between life and death. So what is this idea, this intangible and incomparable concept called love? After all, we are to love our neighbor as ourselves. How do we love others if we do not know how to love ourselves? More importantly what is love?

Love is the life's blood of your purpose. It is what makes you continue with the task at hand when you want to give up. It causes you to go above and beyond and discover strength you never knew resided inside of you. This chapter will define what love is in comparison to what we have made it to be and give a brief overview of the three strands of purpose before we explore them in depth in later chapters.

The Greek word for love found in Mark 12:31, "...You shall love your neighbor as yourself," is agapao, which means to love, esteem, cherish, favor, honor, respect, accept, prize, relish. The world today would be such a different place if we chose to love our neighbor, esteem those who have no self-esteem, cherish the unloved, favor those who have lost all hope, honor those who have been forgotten, respect those who have no respect for themselves, accept those society has rejected, see everyone as a prize rather than expendable, and relish our interactions with others no matter how small or insignificant the interactions may seem.

Notice the definition for love does not have any parameters set. There is no minimum or maximum level. Love just is. It is complete and whole. So to say, "I love you a lot" or "I love you more today than yesterday," we are unintentionally diluting love. Can you truly love someone less and still call it love? If you love someone more today did you really love them yesterday? We need to get to the point where "I love you" carries its full weight at all times.

How does God love us?

Before you can love someone else, you must be able to love you. Do you love you? What is the proper way to love you? In order to answer this we need to know how God loves us. What better person to teach us how to love ourselves than the One who loved us first. 1 John 4:19 reads, "We love Him because He first loved us," and John 3:16-17 reads, "For God so loved the world that He gave His only begotten Son, that whoever believes in Him should not perish but have everlasting life. For God did not send His Son into the world to condemn the world, but that the world through Him might be saved." God's love – pure, unadulterated, undiluted love – is sacrifice.

God is the ultimate parent, the Father of us all. Like any good parent, He has given us instructions, His Word (the Bible), in which to prepare us for the rest of our life on earth and for eternity with Him. Why? Because He loves us and always wants the very best for us. God's instructions are not to harm us or afflict us, but to protect, encourage, correct, and guide. They are not to be seen as rules we begrudgingly follow or a list of how-to's amongst the many not-to's as so many see God's Word. If you did not know it before, love is sacrifice.

How do we love ourselves?

What does loving you look like? Ephesians 5:29 reads, "For no one ever hated his own flesh, but nourishes and cherishes it, just as the Lord does the church." This scripture says that we should love our own body the same way Christ loves the church by feeding and caring for it. How does this apply to how we love ourselves?

Jesus does not feed the church junk, but has provided us with His Word, which is filling, without impurities, and nourishing. In the same way, if we love ourselves, we must also feed our minds and bodies accordingly. When we consume something filling, it can be said that it satisfies our craving or hunger. Do the thoughts and information that you feed your mind satisfy your cravings for knowledge, peace of mind, and motivation or are you left wanting after a day of sitting in front of the television? Does the food that you put in your body fill you up or are you hungry a couple hours later?

Let us also steer clear of all impurities. An impurity is "...an unwanted substance that is found in something else that prevents it from being pure..." (Merriam-Webster). These impurities are typically unwanted and are considered unnecessary and unimportant. What unnecessary dreams and fantasies do you entertain that prevent you from thinking, praying, and speaking clearly and with focus? Are there any impurities in the foods that you put in your body? Perhaps the foods contain a high concentration of preservatives, antibiotics, sugars, salt, etc. that greatly reduce the health benefit of what you are consuming. Instead, take in only that which is nourishing to the mind, body and soul. The word *nourish* is defined as "to provide (someone or something) with food and other things that are needed to live, be healthy, etc...to cause (something) to develop or grow stronger...to promote the growth of..." (Merriam-Webster). If what you read, watch, or discuss with others is not healthy, does not encourage you to grow spiritually or cause you to stretch more in Christ, then you should put it down and leave it alone.

By permission. From Merriam-Webster's Collegiate® Dictionary, 11th Edition ©2016 by Merriam-Webster, Inc. (www.Merriam-Webster.com)

According to Ephesians 5:29, Christ's care of the church is second to none. Jesus is the Great Shepherd. He protects, leads, guides, and disciplines us. Similarly, we too must protect, lead, guide and discipline ourselves. Protect yourself from negative and abusive people and thoughts. Lead yourself, family, and friends using the truths found in the Bible. In everything, let the Word of God guide your prayers and thoughts to reach the goals that God has for you, and discipline your mind and body to reject anything that would be a distraction, cause harm, or become a habit that is contrary to God's Word.

How do we love others?
It is quite simple! Everything mentioned above, do for others. When you speak or interact with your friends, families, coworkers, or strangers be sure you do so without negativity, impurities, profanity, half-truths, empty words, etc., but leave them with the pure unadulterated truths of God. Build up, encourage and motivate wherever you go. Do not leave anyone the same way you found them. Where there is negativity, leave them with a word of encouragement. Where there is chaos, offer them a prayer for peace and direction. Watch your own thoughts and speech. If we protect, lead, guide, and discipline ourselves, what we share and demonstrate to others should reflect the love we have for ourselves and be transferred to them.

What if you smiled at and engaged in conversation the young man whose pants are sagging and always hanging around the neighborhood or that young girl that is always surrounded by young men? Show them some of that loving-kindness that God bestows upon you every day. Show them that someone cares about them as a person, that they are worth the time, and that they are worthy of a smile and soft speech, as opposed to the neglect and harsh tones they may receive at home. Become like

---

By permission. From Merriam-Webster's Collegiate® Dictionary, 11th Edition ©2016 by Merriam-Webster, Inc. (www.Merriam-Webster.com)

the Good Samaritan (Luke 10:25-37). Let us not leave them in the road *half dead* for others to step over, dismiss, and misuse. I know you have seen those horror movies when people have been abused or killed. They come back either as a zombie or serial killer to pay back those responsible and those that did nothing to help them.

Those that work with at-risk youth will tell you it is not protection that makes young men and women join gangs, but love. They are seeking a place where they are loved and accepted. It goes beyond having a family. As some can attest, sometimes our own families do not resemble the loving families seen on television during the era of "Leave It to Beaver" and "The Cosby Show."

Let us nurse those that are *half dead* back to health so they will not have the bitter taste and craving to take the life of another, commit petty crimes, or harm themselves.

Chapter 2 Reflection Questions
1. What is the life's blood of your purpose?
2. How have you unintentionally diluted love?
3. What are some impurities you are feeding your body and mind? How can you nourish your body and mind instead?
4. Think of someone you can show love to that the world has mistreated. Pray that God gives you the opportunity.

CHAPTER 3
LOVING GOD: LEARNING TO LOVE THE PURPOSE-GIVER

It was mentioned in the previous chapters, our purpose first and foremost is to love and be loved while intertwining three elements – God, you, and others. The first strand in finding your purpose is loving God, which we discovered in the first greatest commandment and further illustrated in commandments 1-4 of the Ten Commandments. Although these commandments tell us what to do, there are no specifics on how to accomplish this feat. We know that love comes from God. We are unable to distribute love without receiving it first from Him. In Deuteronomy 6, God tells us how we are to love Him. Before we can do and be what we were created for, we must learn how to love the Purpose-Giver. I have made a list of seven ways we can show God love.

#1 Remember Where You Come From
Deuteronomy 6:10-12
^{10}"So it shall be, when the LORD your God brings you into the land of which He swore to your fathers, to Abraham, Isaac, and Jacob, to give you large and beautiful cities which you did not build, ^{11}houses full of all good things, which you did not dig, vineyards and olive trees which you did not plant – when you have eaten and

are full – ¹²then beware, lest you forget the LORD who brought you out of the land of Egypt, from the house of bondage."

In the text, God promised the Israelites, who had not yet reached the Promise Land, that He would give them the land He had promised Abraham, Isaac, and Jacob. However, the cities they would inherit will have belonged to another people so when they take possession they will find move-in ready dwellings filled with many amenities. They will not have to furnish the houses or plant any crops. God warns them that although they would be blessed with all of these things, they must not forget their humble beginnings or who their God is. It is the relationship that God had with their forefathers, that enabled them to benefit from a great promise finally to be fulfilled.

Likewise, if we were to look at our own lives, some blessings we have are not due to anything we have done, but what those before us have done. I don't know about you, but have you been at a store or venue where nobody knows who you are? Suddenly out of the blue, someone stops you and asks, "Are you so-and-so's daughter, son, granddaughter, or grandson?" It is from the relationship they have or had with your parents or grandparents that you were blessed with a kind word, a gift, or an unexpected opportunity. The favor shown to you was not something you earned, but it was provided by the reputation and hard work of those that came before you. It is only because of God's favor that these blessings have trickled down to you. You are to love the Lord your God. Do not forget where He has brought you from and how He has blessed you beyond what you deserve.

#2 Respect, Serve, and Don't Make Promises You Can't Keep
Deuteronomy 6:13
¹³"You shall fear the LORD your God and serve Him, and shall take oaths in His name."

The first part of verse 13 simply means, we are to have reverential awe toward God. In other words, we are to display honor and respect. How do we show honor and respect to others? Take for example, when we enter our grandparents' home or supervisor's office, we check all attitudes at the door, offer our service to assist, bring any issues confidently but with emotions under control, and we do not get ahead of them trying to finish their sentences or leave before being dismissed. Do we enter the presence of God and His house with this same honor and respect?

There are many times we may have woke up on the wrong side of the bed and dragged ourselves to church with a chip on our shoulder. There are others who enter the church not wanting to serve, but only to be served. They do not want to be asked to hand out programs or greet visitors, but prefer to sit glued to their seat throughout the entire worship service undisturbed. In our prayer time, when we do not understand a decision God made to not answer our prayer the way we would like, we may have lashed out angrily at God. Instead of asking for peace or understanding, we attack the only One who is truly in our corner. Prayer is a two-way street. Once you have finished praying, do you rush to get up and leave before receiving God's response? All of these things are disrespectful to God, His nature, and His house.

Once we receive our orders from God we are to serve Him only. That means everything we do should serve God. For those who have siblings, did you know that by helping your brother or sister, you were in turn helping out your parents? Think about it. If you did not help them tie their shoe or do their homework, who would it fall on? Your mom or your dad. I remember my mother telling me to help her by helping my sister. In the same way, when we serve and go that extra mile for one another, we are serving God. We are an extension of God and become His hands and feet.

At first glance, the declaration in the second part of verse 13 looks strange. If you recall from the Ten Commandments, we are not to take God's name in vain, however, we now read we are to "take oaths in His name." What does this mean? This is not a contradiction. The last part of the verse 13 is saying that if we make any promises they are to be in God's name. Why? To do so carelessly and not to fulfill that promise would show irreverence and disrespect to God. To make our promises in the name of God would hold us accountable to God and should make us think twice before making promises we have no intention of keeping. You are to love the Lord your God. Respect God, serve Him only, and do not carelessly make promises.

#3 Be Faithful to God
Deuteronomy 6:14-15
14You shall not go after other gods, the gods of the peoples who are all around you; 15(for the LORD your God is a jealous God among you), lest the anger of the LORD your God be aroused against you and destroy you from the face of the earth."

Plain and simple, do not let the company you keep change your character and draw you away from God. When you hang around certain friends, family members, or co-workers, does your mood or character change? Do you find yourself using profanity, lying, or short-tempered? What effect does it have on your priorities? Don't let staying out late on a Saturday night with your friends keep you in the bed on Sunday morning. If someone asked you if you had to choose would you rather be late to work or late to church, what would you say? Don't let the temptation to live in a moment, overshadow the importance of where you will spend eternity. God is a jealous God, intolerant of unfaithfulness and His anger will be aroused against you. You are to love the Lord your God. Follow no other gods and put no one or nothing before Him.

#4 Don't Shoot the Messenger
Deuteronomy 6:16
16"You shall not tempt the LORD your God as you tempted Him in Massah."

The meaning of this verse is not easily deciphered. You must first know the history of Massah. In Exodus 17, the Israelites tested God. They were thirsty and complained loudly to Moses so much that he thought they would stone him if God did not supply them with water. You might be asking, "How does quarreling with Moses equate to tempting God?" Moses was God's mouthpiece, His messenger. The people were threatening to proverbially shoot the messenger.

We need to define a couple words to get a full understanding of what was actually happening. Tempt is another word for provoke. Quarrel has many synonyms, such as, hassle, argue, bicker, or fall out. The Israelites argued with Moses so harshly that they provoked God to action. They challenged God to show Himself. Exodus 17:7 reads, "So he [Moses] called the name of the place Massah and Meribah, because of the contention of the children of Israel, and because they tempted the LORD, saying, 'Is the LORD among us or not?'" The nerve of the Israelites to demand God to show Himself and relentlessly heckle His messenger.

In modern times, this verse still applies. We are to not hassle or argue with the angel, messenger, or as we call him, pastor, of the church. He is leading according to the commands and orders God has given him. When we fall out and argue with the pastor and what he is teaching, we are actually falling out and arguing with God because He is the one that sent the message. You are to love the Lord your God. Do not quarrel with His messengers.

#5 Just Do What God Says

Deuteronomy 6:17-19
17"You shall diligently keep the commandments of the LORD your God, His testimonies, and His statues which He has commanded you. 18And you shall do what is right and good in the sight of the LORD, that it may be well with you, and that you may go in and possess the good land of which the LORD swore to your fathers, 19to cast out all your enemies from before you, as the LORD has spoken."

These verses are cut and dry. We are to obey the orders, requirements, and decisions God has given us. Do what is right and good in His sight, not your own sight, so that He may do all that He promised. In addition, your enemies will be cast out, or thrown out forcefully before you. Those enemies that are hiding amongst your friends will be made known to you and they will be unable to hinder or delay the blessings God has for you. All God is asking is for you obey Him. In John 14:15, Jesus said, "If you love Me, keep My commandments." How many can think of a time when had we obeyed our parents we could have avoided a consequence or two, such as, heartache, loss of money, ego, prized possession, etc.? God loves you and only has your best interest at heart. Just do what He says.

#6 Share About the Goodness of Your God
Deuteronomy 6:20-23
[20]"When your son asks you in time to come, saying, 'What is the meaning of the testimonies, the statutes, and the judgments which the LORD our God has commanded you?' [21]then you shall say to your son: 'We were slaves of Pharaoh in Egypt, and the LORD brought us out of Egypt with a mighty hand; [22]and the LORD showed signs and wonders before our eyes, great and severe, against Egypt, Pharaoh, and all his household. [23]Then He brought us out from there, that He might bring us in, to give us the land of which He swore to our fathers.'"

God is saying a lot in this passage. First, there will be descendants. The Israelites will not become extinct or wiped out by whatever obstacle or battle is in their future, but will be blessed with children. Second, it is their responsibility to tell their children about God, His testimonies, statutes, and judgments and explain what they mean. It is one thing to tell someone the facts and another thing to explain why and how to give them understanding. Third, the Israelites were to tell their children where they came from, what lifestyle and situation God had delivered them, and how He did so. They were to tell of a great, powerful God who rescued His people from one of the strongest nations on earth. Lastly, they were to tell their children of God's faithfulness to deliver on His promises. For we know that God does not lie

(Numbers 23:19).

Today, are we doing what God has commanded? Are we telling others about Him, teaching them His commandments, reading the testimonies of those in the Bible, and warning them of God's past judgments on those who were disobedient? Do we tell our children, cousins, nieces, or nephews where God has brought us from and what situations or mistakes He has rescued us from? It could be from an abusive relationship, making a bad decision in high school that could have negatively affected your academic career or given you a criminal record, or the grips of unforgiveness giving you the strength to finally forgive. You should not want anyone to repeat your mistakes. If you can help them avoid these mistakes, please do.

As a society, we are so desensitized to bad news that we sometimes forget to turn our focus to the good in the world. Remind yourself, your children, and those you witness to of God's faithfulness to fulfill His promises. Tell them of how God came through for you in the nick of time. There's a song that says, *"He may not come when you want Him, but* He'll be there *right on time."* Many can attest to this truth. Tell someone about your God. When you love someone you can't help but tell others about them, how they make you feel, and what they've done for you. Share about the goodness of your God.

#7 Observe All These Commandments
Deuteronomy 6:24-25
²⁴"And the LORD commanded us to observe all these statutes, to fear the LORD our God, for our good always, that He might preserve us alive, as it is this day. ²⁵Then it will be righteousness for us, if we are careful to observe all these commandments before the LORD, our God, as He has commanded us."

In these last two verses, we read again that God has our best interest at heart. His commands are "for our good always that He might preserve us alive." Merriam-Webster defines *preserve* as "to keep (something) in its original state or in good condition…" and

"...to keep (something) safe from harm or loss." If we keep God's commandments, respect and reverence Him, He will always protect us and ensure everything is for our good. Even when things do not seem to go according to how we think they should, we must trust and believe that whatever the outcome it is for our good (Romans 8:28). In saying that, we must not skip over the small three-letter word *all* that is mentioned twice. We must be attentive and cautious to follow *all* that He has commanded us. We cannot pick and choose which rules to follow when we are driving on the highway, so why do we think it is okay to break a few rules with God. Our purpose is to love God and to be loved by Him. To love Him is to obey Him (John 14:15). All of His instructions are for our good and are not designed to cause us harm or distress.

This list of seven ways how to love God is not an exhaustive list, but it is a good place to start. The more we examine God's Word, the more we learn how to love Him. I hope this chapter helped shed light on how we are to love God. Our focus first and foremost should be on Him. Loving God is the biggest part of your purpose. You were born because God loves you and wants to show you love. You cannot truly love you and the purpose God has for you until you learn to accept who you are. That begins with learning how to love the Purpose-Giver.

God loves each of us. He sent His son, Jesus, to die on the cross. He gave *His* Son for *you*. All He wants is your love in return. He is not asking you to do any tricks to show Him that you love Him. He wants us to be appreciative, respectful, eager to serve, accountable for our actions (not blaming anyone else), faithful, to go along with His flow, not buck and try to test Him through His messengers, and to be obedient to all He has commanded. If we do *all* these things He will bless us and we will triumph over our enemies.

By permission. From Merriam-Webster's Collegiate® Dictionary, 11th Edition ©2016 by Merriam-Webster, Inc. (www.Merriam-Webster.com)

Chapter 3 Reflection Questions

1. Reflect on where God has brought you from and how He has blessed you beyond what you deserve.
2. Do you sometimes enter the presence of God in prayer or His house (church) with an attitude, distracted by your cell phone, etc.? Do you make promises you have no intention of keeping?
3. What people or things sometimes come between you and God? (reasons you put off praying, going to church, etc.)
4. Have you ever been angry at something the pastor has done or said? Did you gossip to others or did you go directly to God in prayer to seek His understanding or wisdom on how to respond?
5. No one is perfect. We all are disobedient at times, choosing to do what we want instead of what we know God wants us to do. What is one thing you know God wants you to do that you have not done?
6. Do you share with others the goodness of God?
7. Pray to God for help in obeying all of His commands and that you remain aware of where you stand in regard to questions #1-6. Ask for God's guidance.

CHAPTER 4
LOVING YOU: YOU ARE WORTH IT

The second strand in finding your purpose is loving you. So many give up on life, love, being happy, having a family, reaching goals, etc. because they look over their life and they want to know if this is it. Is this all that life is about? Why am I here? What significant role do I play at this point in time to the people in my life? Am I aiming above or below my potential?

There are three parts to loving you: self-awareness, self-acceptance, and self-love.

Self-Awareness: Are you aware of your current condition?
Philippians 4:10-13
[10]But I rejoiced in the Lord greatly that now at last your care for me has flourished again; though you surely did care, but you lacked opportunity. [11]Not that I speak in regard to need, for I have learned in whatever state I am, to be content: [12]I know how to be abased, and I know how to abound. Everywhere and in all things I have learned both to be full and to be hungry, both to abound and to suffer need. [13]I can do all things through Christ who strengthens me.

Self-awareness is defined as "...knowledge and awareness of

one's own personality or character..." (Merriam-Webster). This also includes your feelings, motives, and desires.

How aware are we of our mental and emotional state? So many people deal with depression, drug use, addiction, alcoholism, etc. We are numbing ourselves from what? Pain, heartache, worry, drowning in self-pity, overwhelmed by emotions. Some of us may not numb ourselves with narcotics, but surround ourselves with people constantly. Some cannot sit in the house alone or ride in the car with the radio turned off. They have to constantly be moving and be the life of the party, workplace, or classroom. They have to keep their environment stirred up and their audience either laughing at their antics or instigating their enemies to fight.

When we find ourselves alone and the focus is just on us, our world has just been shrunk. We become so small and insignificant that sometimes we do not notice or recognize the size of our God, the might of His power, or the great reach of His love. We blindly step over and push past those around us because we think they just do not and cannot understand what we are going through.

How does God put things back in perspective? One way is He brings others into our lives for us to help, pray for, and focus on to get the focus off of self. It is then we are able to forget about our problems and after we finish our task of ministering to another individual, we find that our problem really was not as big as we thought and God has already taken care of it. A second way is God will isolate you from others to force you to face *you*, and to see and lean upon Him alone. In one instance, God uses us to bless others as He corrects and redirects our own misguided feelings, motives and desires. In the other instance, God forces us to no longer be in denial to our current state and surrender to Him.

Do not be afraid to look in the mirror. Examine yourself. Be conscious of your character (personality and temperament), feelings (emotional state), motives (reason for doing things), and

---

By permission. From Merriam-Webster's Collegiate® Dictionary, 11th Edition ©2016 by Merriam-Webster, Inc. (www.Merriam-Webster.com)

desires (wishes and dreams). Recognize your mood swings – both the ups and downs. Learn to be content in all circumstances, which can only be accomplished through faith. Know you can do all things through Christ who strengthens you. When times get hard or life gets you down, re-read Philippians 4:10-13, commit it to memory and stand on its truth.

You must love you. You are worth it.

Self-acceptance: God Made No Mistakes When He Made You
Exodus 4:10-12
[10]Then Moses said to the LORD, "O my Lord, I am not eloquent, neither before nor since You have spoken to Your servant; but I am slow of speech and slow of tongue." [11]So the LORD said to him, "Who has made man's mouth? Or who makes the mute, the deaf, the seeing, or the blind? Have not I, the LORD? [12]Now therefore, go, and I will be with your mouth and teach you what you shall say."

Self-acceptance is the acceptance of self in spite of deficiencies. I can identify with Moses in more ways than one. I, too, stutter and God has called me to preach His Word. From my perspective, having a moderate to severe stutter depending on my stress level is bad enough. It is frustrating when you have something to say, but cannot quite communicate as fluent or effortlessly as one would prefer. Then add the stress of speaking in front of others and one can see why Moses asked God to pick someone else. To Moses (and me), it just felt like too much. The point is we all have deficiencies. We all have something we would like to do better or change. Often times, we may even feel our deficiencies will keep us from serving God or that He cannot use us. That is not true. God made each of us. He knows our strengths and our weaknesses. Whatever purpose God has for us our deficiencies do not pose a threat to His will being done. What we feel is a negative God can turn it and use it for good.

Another deficiency I had as a child was a very short temper

and fighting came second nature. One day my mother left me and my sister alone with our uncle. I was around 10 or 11 years old and my sister was 3 or 4 years old. In the time my mother was gone, my sister had gone into my room and took something. It made me angry. I chased her down the hall and attacked her. In my head, I thought I would feel better getting her back, but that was not the case. I had hurt the one person I had told myself I would protect. That day I prayed. I told God I never wanted to hurt anyone like that again and asked Him to teach me to fight for Him.

My sister and I are 7 years and three months apart. I was young. I didn't know what I had really prayed. I did not realize it until I went to college when I began to grow as a prayer warrior. God redirected what some might consider a deficiency – my short fuse and willingness to fight on a dime. Oddly enough, I could have asked God to change me and remove my desire to fight, but in my youth I did not think anything was wrong with how I was made. I just asked God to use my desire for His glory so that it would be pleasing to Him. God did modify things – my fuse is a lot longer in hostile situations and I take my fight to the Lord.

What deficiency do you have that you think God cannot use? Accept all of you. God did not make any mistakes when He made you. God can redirect and refocus your insecurities when you decide to be secure in Him.

You must love you. You are worth it.

Self-love: Don't Be Afraid, Guilty, or Too Lazy to Love Yourself
Proverbs 4:23-27
²³ Keep your heart with all diligence,
  For out of it spring the issues of life.
²⁴ Put away from you a deceitful mouth,
  And put perverse lips far from you.
²⁵ Let your eyes look straight ahead;
  And your eyelids look right before you.
²⁶ Ponder the path of your feet,
  And let all your ways be established.

²⁷ *Do not turn to the right or the left;*
  Remove your foot from evil.

Self-love is defined as "...regard for one's own happiness or advantage..." (Merriam-Webster). If you love yourself, what do you do? You eat healthy, make sure you have a roof over your head, wear a seat belt, surround yourself with people that mean you good and not harm, the list goes on. Basically, you guard and preserve yourself and defend yourself from harm. That means from all physical, mental and emotional calamity. You should be on the defensive when it comes to your own well-being.

If you are not on the defensive, you are not loving you. Are you letting people upset you and constantly hang around in your circle that have no right to be there? Are you ingesting harmful chemicals in the form of drugs, alcohol or foods saturated in man-made preservatives, high in fat, sodium and cholesterol? Are you living an inactive lifestyle where you are eating more calories than you are burning? Are you listening to toxic music that gets you revved up and ready to fight the next person that looks at you wrong or brings you so low you find yourself depressed and feeling like you have no fruitful future? Are you in relationships that seem to be headed nowhere fast in which you are giving more than you are receiving? Do you feel beat up, worn and tired in their presence rather than rejuvenated, strong and joyful? If you answered yes to any of those questions, stop and protect yourself.

Also, keep in mind there are times you have to protect you from you in the same manner you protect yourself from those around you. Do not forget you are *supposed* to love you. Keep and guard your heart. Everything you do reflects the condition of your heart. The words that leave your mouth should be helpful and not self-deprecating or critical, truthful and not dishonest. The longer we live a lie, the harder it is to face reality. Focus on the future and what is ahead, not the what ifs and regrets of yesterday. Think

---

By permission. From Merriam-Webster's Collegiate® Dictionary, 11th Edition ©2016 by Merriam-Webster, Inc. (www.Merriam-Webster.com)

before you act and stand firm on Proverbs 4:23-27. Protect yourself.

You must love you. You are worth it.

Jesus was born for you. Jesus was whipped and hung on the cross for you. Jesus bled and died for you. Jesus got up after three days and three nights for you. I hope you have accepted Jesus as your Savior. He lives and is preparing a place in heaven for you at this moment. Jesus loves you and you are worth it. Complete self-awareness, self-acceptance, and self-love is not possible without Jesus. It is time we all believe and walk in that truth.

Chapter 4 Reflection Questions
1. What is your current physical, mental, or emotional condition? Are you in pain, depressed, or is something stressing you? Are you happy or full of joy?
2. What deficiencies do you have that you think God cannot use?
3. In what areas could you be more defensive and protective of yourself?
4. What are some truths (scriptures) you will commit to memory, stick to your mirror, or carry with you to recite aloud to crush any negative words and thoughts? Write them out on a piece of paper and place where you can get to it easily.

CHAPTER 5
LOVING OTHERS: MAKING DISCIPLES

We are still talking about God's purpose for your life. It is not mystical or beyond your reach. I cannot say it enough, the only way to discover and fulfill your purpose is to love.

Let's Review

In Chapter 1, we defined purpose. We came to the conclusion everything we do should be on purpose and with intention. We also discovered the simple answer to the question of our purpose was to love and be loved according to 1 John 4:8. Before we can do and be what we were created for, we must learn how to Love God who is the Purpose-Giver. There are seven ways to love God, which you can refer back to Chapter 3. We discovered in Chapter 4 that there are three parts to loving you:
    1) Self-awareness
    2) Self-acceptance
    3) Self-love

Finally, we have come to the third and final strand of our purpose -- loving others.

Congratulations! You've made it!

You have salvation and escaped the fate of being separated from God. Now what? Well, who else is going to heaven with you? Have you invited any friends or family? What about a coworker or your favorite cashier at the grocery store? You have come all this way through your journey in life. God gave you the victory time after time and what do you have to show for it? Did you go back and tell anyone else?

Luke 22:31-32 reads, And the Lord said, "Simon, Simon! Indeed, Satan has asked for you, that he may sift you as wheat. But I have prayed for you, that your faith should not fail; and when you have returned to Me, strengthen your brethren." Jesus wants our faith to remain strong and that we would strengthen one another.

We are all God's creation. He loves us all, everyone in every city, state, country, continent, and in the world (John 3:16-17). He does not want you, me, or anyone else to perish. If we love God, we obey His commands (John 14:23-24). One of the commands given to everyone who has accepted our Lord and Savior is the Great Commission found in Matthew 28:18-20 which reads, "And Jesus came and spoke to them, saying, 'All authority has been given to Me in heaven and on earth. Go therefore and make disciples of all the nations, baptizing them in the name of the Father and of the Son and of the Holy Spirit, teaching them to observe all things that I have commanded you; and lo I am with you always, even to the end of the age.' Amen." Are you making disciples?

What is a disciple?

A disciple is a learner, follower, or one who studies under the instruction of a teacher. It can be said that it takes a disciple to make a disciple because you never stop being a disciple or follower of Christ. We should always be in the posture of both teaching and learning.

What does it mean to disciple?

When you disciple someone it goes beyond teaching and sharing information. You have the opportunity to shape their character and how they see the world through a close, personal relationship. You cannot be hands off and stand at a distance. You have to get to know who you are discipling.

The Bible tells us we are to love God, love ourselves, and love our neighbors as ourselves. Do you want to go to hell? Or to be eternally separated from God? Then neither should we want anyone else to suffer that fate. That includes our enemies.

In Matthew 18:12-14, Jesus asks, "What do you think? If a man has a hundred sheep, and one of them goes astray, does he not leave the ninety-nine and go to the mountains to seek the one that is straying? And if he should find it, assuredly, I say to you, he rejoices more over the sheep than over the ninety-nine that did not go astray. Even so it is not the will of your Father who is in heaven that one of these little ones should perish." Jesus cares for everyone. Even if you were the only one lost in sin, He would have still got on the cross for you. We have to ask ourselves: Are we holding on too tightly and selfishly to that grudge, pride, position, or our time that we are willing to see our aunt, uncle, cousin, coworker, or the mean lady at the gas station miss out on the opportunity to go to heaven?

Why Should We Make Disciples?

This book is about one thing: love. When you surrender your heart first to God, you can love yourself and anyone else including your worse enemy. No matter how great someone's sin in our eyes or the quantity of their sins, we still must love. We must not react the way the world does with revenge. Paul writes in Romans 12:19-21, "Beloved, do not avenge yourselves, but rather give place to wrath; for it is written, 'Vengeance is Mine, I will repay,' says the Lord. Therefore 'If your enemy is hungry, feed him; If he is thirsty, give him a drink; For in so doing you will heap coals of fire on his head.' Do not be overcome by evil, but overcome evil with good."

We must pray to God that He blesses our enemies (Luke 6:27-31). Even on your worse day when you do not deserve it, wouldn't you want someone to still hope and believe good things for you?

After all, when tomorrow comes it is another chance to get it right, to apologize, and repent.

If you are not making disciples, what are you doing? What greater love can you show someone than to bring someone else into relationship and fellowship with the One that loves them the most? What greater love can you show God, than by bringing one of His children to Him? Your enemy would become your friend. You would not have to keep looking over your shoulder. You would not have to keep your purse or wallet in the car when you go over that relative's house. Just think how many precautions we would not have to take if we had brothers and sisters everywhere we went that actually *lived* for Christ and we held each other accountable for our actions in and outside of the church because we were true disciples.

How Do You Make Disciples?

First and foremost, before you can make a disciple, you must be a disciple. In order to follow, believe, and listen to the voice and words of God, you must read, memorize, and study the Bible. Do not forget your first purpose is to love God. You must worship Christ, pray, fast, and obey His commands. It is important that we share God's love and witness to unbelievers. Look for opportunities and engage them in conversation. Be sure you find a church that teaches the Bible and become active in a ministry. Find out where and how you can serve the body of Christ. We are all called to go beyond the four walls of the church. You can get involved in, pray for, and give to international missions that serve other nations, such as, The Voice of Martyrs. After you have done all the above look around your circle for those you can disciple. Choose a few people to spend time with, teach them from God's word, and be a model of what true obedience to Christ is. For a complete personal disciple-making plan, I recommend David Platt's book, *Follow Me*.

Go and Live Out Your Purpose

What is your purpose? Love. How? I have given seven ways to

love God, three ways to love yourself, and one way to love others. Each of those can be illustrated in multiple ways. We should never wake up with nothing to do. Each day is a new opportunity to show love. What is a skill or a dream you have always had? Is there a way to use it to show love to God, yourself, and others?

Never stop learning to love the Purpose-Giver.
Never stop believing you are worth being loved.
Never stop making disciples.
Never stop loving.

Remember that love is an action. It is a choice. I pray you choose to love.

Chapter 5 Reflection Questions
1. Have you told anyone in your family or social circle about Christ and His gift of salvation?
2. Are you discipling anyone? Why not?
3. List three people you can disciple.
4. Pray to God to create an opportunity for you to disciple those on your list or bring someone to you to disciple.

CHAPTER 6
KEEP LOVE FOREVER PRESENT

To not show love has the potential of creating or perpetuating an existing cycle of pain, frustration, confusion, or animosity in our own lives as well as those we interact with in that manner. That is why showing others love, as opposed to revenge, is so important. Not only does it allow us to give outside of ourselves, add to the life of someone else, and enrich our own heart in return, but it is one of the greatest commandments given by God. By loving others, we are showing our love for God. In John 14:15, 21, Jesus says, "If you love Me, keep My commandments...He who has My commandments and keeps them, it is he who loves Me. And he who loves Me will be loved by My Father, and I will love him and manifest Myself to him." To not love the person working in the next cubicle, the driver in the car in front of you, or the child that just trampled your garden, is an offense against God. Keep love forever present and never absent from your heart.

    We all know what happens when love is absent. We are left with the me-society of today that is displayed on the news and in the actions of those we see at the grocery store during snowstorm warnings and mall on Black Friday. Selfishness runs rampant. There is a disregard for others and carelessness in regard to human life. It is not uncommon to almost get closed in a door because the person before you did not hold it open. We can turn on the TV and see road rage that ends in a lost life, the death of a child at the hands of a parent or grandparent, teens killing because they were bored, teachers molesting students, criminals stealing the retirement of the elderly, drunk drivers continuously choosing to drive drunk, drug dealers producing illegal drugs that look appealing to young children, the list goes on. This is what happens when there is no love. The opposite of love is not hate, but indifference.

Let us stop watching the news or reading the headlines with a dismissive shake of our head and indifference. We should be compelled to move and act. With all the violence happening today, ask yourself, Is there enough love to counteract it? Am I doing what I can by showing love to those I cross paths? To be indifferent and do nothing is to watch the world slip faster and further into depravity.

Do Not Perpetuate the Cycle

Never, no matter how much you are pushed, should we pay back evil for evil. We know the consequences of what getting even gets you — nothing but more evil. What happens when one gang kills the member of another? What happens when they get the offending gang back? Does the killing end or does it continue to go back and forth?

Paul writes in Galatians 5:15, "But if you bite and devour one another, beware lest you be consumed by one another!" When a person or animal bites, it wounds or pierces the flesh of another. Paul's warns the Christians in Galatia that once someone initiates a bite, others will be drawn into the attack until there is nothing left of all those involved.

Paul even took it a step further and added the word devour, which means to greedily eat without inhibition. He was saying that instead of showing each other love, the Galatians were wounding and piercing one another possibly with both their words and deeds. This constant attack on one another was leading them to destroy each other and they enjoyed doing it. When you think of a lion devouring its prey you can visualize it eagerly pouncing on a defenseless animal and eating it until there is nothing left. There may have been times when you attacked someone weaker than you or that you did not like, either physically or verbally, and you did not let up until there was nothing left of their character or pride. Looking back, you know this was not pleasing to God.

Just as in the animal kingdom where the smallest drop of blood can create a frenzy, the smallest painful criticism or media hype can cause us to attack one another. Think about when a celebrity, such as Brittany Spears, Michael Jackson, Miley Cyrus, or Whitney Houston, demonstrated questionable behavior how quick we were to attack and jump to conclusions. Like piranha we may have joined in the fray to rip apart their character, dismantle what is left of their self-esteem, and smother what little hope they held.

If we continue to wound and destroy others, do not think our time will not come. You have heard the phrase "live by the sword die by the sword." We have modernized it to "live by the gun, die by the gun." In essence, it means if you use violence against others eventually you will also meet the same fate. Jesus said the exact same thing in Matthew 26:52 to the companion that cut off the ear of the servant of the high priest, "...Put your sword in its place, for all who take the sword will perish by the sword." Violence, like love, is cyclical. What goes around comes around. Let us use our teeth for smiling not biting and reach out to help each other up rather than destroy. Love your neighbor.

Love is Contagious – Share It

Love is contagious. Share it with everyone you meet. Give a smile as you walk around your workplace, hold the door open, help someone pick up fallen papers, check on the elderly in your neighborhood throughout the week, organize a block party or game night to get to know your neighbors, or invite people you meet while you are out shopping to your church. Do not just talk about it, be about it. Love on purpose. Plain and simple.

Chapter 6 Reflection Questions

1. Have you or are you currently perpetuating violence, exchanging negative words and actions, or planning how to get someone back?
2. Nothing good can come of violence or negativity. Pray that God will give you the strength to respond in love to everyone, including any enemies. Ask for your love to overcome and change the hearts of those you come in contact with.

ABOUT THE AUTHOR

Tyson Canty, a native of Kansas City, Missouri, is a licensed minister at Grace & Mercy Christian Church in Lenexa, Kansas, where she serves in the media ministry; Christian education; outreach development; and as Director of Operations, under the leadership of her husband, Pastor E. F. Canty. She has a passion for creating Sunday School curriculum and Bible studies, along with using various media to share God's Word. A graduate of the University of Missouri-Columbia and University of Missouri-Kansas City, she holds degrees in architectural studies and English. She works as a computer-aided drafter and freelance graphic designer.

www.ingramcontent.com/pod-product-compliance
Lightning Source LLC
Chambersburg PA
CBHW072114290426
44110CB00014B/1914